Re-imagining security

Alastair Crooke, Beverley Milton-Edwards,
Mary Kaldor, Paul Vallely

With an introduction by
James Kennedy

Series editor
Rosemary Bechler

GW00770996

First published 2004
British Council
10 Spring Gardens
London SW1A 2BN
www.britishcouncil.org

Cover design by Atelier Works

Contents

Preface
by the Director-General

The British Council seeks to build long-term relationships between people of different cultures. Our currency is trust. The British Council has been a leader in cultural relations since its founding in 1934. In order to celebrate our 70th anniversary, I asked Counterpoint, our think tank on cultural relations, to commission a series of ten sets of essays, each set looking at a central issue from a variety of angles and viewpoints. The issues range from European enlargement to 'Britishness', and from the significance of death to the role of faith and the nature of secularism.

The 34 writers come from all over the world, though at least one in each set is British. Each introduction, with one exception, is written by a member of British Council staff. They testify to the richness of the intellectual and moral resource that the British Council represents.

Our intention is to stimulate debate rather than arrive at consensus. Some essays are controversial. None of them expresses, individually, a British Council viewpoint. They are the work of individual authors of distinction from whom we have sought views. But collectively, they represent something more than the sum of their parts – a commitment to the belief that dialogue is the essential heart of cultural relations.

Dialogue requires and generates trust. The biggest danger in what is often called public diplomacy work is that we simply broadcast views, policies, values and positions. A senior European diplomat recently said at a British Council conference: 'The world is fed up with hearing us talk. What it wants is for us to shut up and listen.' Listening and demonstrating our commitment to the free and creative interplay of ideas is an indispensable pre-condition for building trust.

To build trust we must engage in effective, open dialogue. Increased mutual understanding based on trust, whether we agree or disagree, is a precious outcome.

David Green KCMG

Introduction
James Kennedy

'The best lack all conviction, while the worst
Are full of passionate intensity.'
W. B. Yeats, 'The Second Coming'

How can an understanding of culture contribute to enhanced
security? What relevance does the soft science of cultural analysis
have to the hard business of protection from the terrorist threat,
which usually involves law enforcement, intelligence gathering, and
military action? Quite a lot, the authors of the three papers in this
booklet would argue. For 'it is evident', writes Mary Kaldor in another
article ('First lessons from Spain', *www.pendemocracy.net*), 'that the
"war on terrorism" is not working.' It is not working, not as a result of
a lack of military muscle, or sense of purpose, or even due to the
'collective failure of intelligence' – but because of a collective failure
of imagination. If we could begin to apply the gentle art of listening
and the soft skills of cultural understanding to the security problems
the world is currently facing, we might avoid what Mary Kaldor calls
the 'series of terrible mistakes' that characterise the current
approach.

Beverley Milton-Edwards and Alastair Crooke take as their
starting point the cultural conflict between Western secular
modernity on the one hand, and political Islam on the other. Crooke,
who spent six years in the Middle East as security adviser to the EU
High Representative Javier Solana, has elsewhere spoken out for a
dialogue with radical groups like Hamas. Here the authors propose a
dialogue between the adversaries, where those involved 'must listen

in a way that allows their own values to be challenged, and where necessary, modified'. Current Western attempts to bring the benefits of civilisation, freedom and democracy to 'backward' Islamic countries are rejected by political Islam, which sees only a neo-colonialist agenda in our international interventions, and moral degradation and social breakdown in our consumption-driven societies. Without an effective dialogue, the spiral of misunderstanding and violence will continue.

Paul Vallely offers a very different, but not incompatible, perspective on the Western–Muslim cultural divide. His article traces a powerful strand of resurgent Christian fundamentalism running through the strategic thinking of the current US administration. It is not so much Western secularism (as Milton-Edwards and Crooke would have it) that is set out in opposition to political Islam, but a radical new interpretation of the Bible, particularly the Old Testament and the Book of Revelation. This sees as its goal the restoration of a greater state of Israel as the necessary precursor to the second coming of Christ. As unreasonable as this may seem to the secular mind, the fundamentalist reapplication of ancient religious texts to modern geo-political conflicts reflects a similar approach in extreme Islam. That both sides in the current conflict should be willing Armageddon as the final solution to the 'war on terror' is scary indeed.

Mary Kaldor bases her arguments on recent interviews in Iraq, and her previous visits to the Balkans and other conflict zones. She uses her own definitions of 'new and old wars' to argue that in new wars, such as Iraq, there can never be a military victory. A political victory may be possible, but only if it is based on bridging the gulfs of cultural understanding between the protagonists. While the military occupiers of Iraq and the Provisional Government stay in the high security 'Green Zone' in Baghdad, and do not engage in dialogue with groups or individuals in the 'Red Zone', the real Iraq, it is unlikely that the huge culture gap can ever be breached. Professor Kaldor proposes a re-imagining of European security, and a new, international, human security force.

This book is not intended as a critique of current US policy on terrorism and security, but rather to explore what role cultural dialogue might play in addressing the security issues faced by the world. That the authors are all critical of the USA is a result of their own research, and their observations that people feel less secure the longer the war on terrorism continues in its current form. But those prosecuting the war show no signs of changing course. By bizarre coincidence a major apologist for the war camp is also called Paul Vallely, retired Major-General in the US army, and senior military adviser to Fox News. In a recent book (*Endgame: The Blueprint for Victory in the War on Terror*) he argues that in order for the USA to be successful in the war on terror, it needs to advance militarily on other nations implicated as 'terrorist-harbourers', including Syria, North Korea, Iran and Libya. It is military might and the 'will to fight' that will bring security to the USA, in a battle in which dialogue and understanding have no role.

The war parties on both sides have the loudest voices, while our authors, and others like them, struggle to be heard. While governments are willing to spend billions of dollars and hundreds of their own soldiers' (and thousands of non-combatants') lives in an unwinnable war, it is left to a few under-funded international organisations, some faith groups and NGOs to argue the case for dialogue and reconciliation.

Regime change in the West would not necessarily make much difference. Writing about a prospective John Kerry presidency, journalist Simon Tisdall, writing in *The Guardian*, comments: 'On terrorism, WMD proliferation and defence . . . Kerry is bent on hanging tough with the toughest, promising – in sum – to prosecute the same, endless, unconfined "war" that Bush declared after 9/11 while somehow rendering it more acceptable to Muslims and Europeans.' In Britain the Liberal Democrats, who have won votes in recent by-elections as a result of their principled stand against the invasion of Iraq, have neither much hope of forming the next government, nor a coherent alternative to the current government's support for US policies.

Nor is there a consistency of alternative thinking on security policy and strategy among those European governments that (largely for individual, domestic political reasons) opposed the invasion of Iraq. Russia, critically weakened since the collapse of the Soviet Union, has its own war on terrorism to prosecute in Chechnya, and its own version of resurgent Christian fundamentalist thinking based on the Orthodox doctrine of Moscow as the Third Rome.

So how can we imagine an alternative approach to security, based on mutuality and cultural dialogue? At the highest level, there is a need for transnational security structures that would bring all the governments involved together. This might start with a dialogue between existing groupings: the EU or the Organisation for Security and Co-operation in Europe (OSCE) on the one side, the Arab League or Organisation of the Islamic Conference (OIC) on the other. In the longer term this could lead to the development of a new security organisation, modelled on the principles of the OSCE: 'The OSCE approach to security is comprehensive and co-operative: comprehensive in dealing with a wide range of security-related issues including arms control, preventive diplomacy, confidence- and security-building measures, human rights, democratization, election monitoring and economic and environmental security; co-operative in the sense that all OSCE participating States have equal status, and decisions are based on consensus.' If the nations of Ronald Reagan's 'Evil Empire' could eventually join the West to tackle security concerns in this way, then why should we not imagine and create a future where George W. Bush's 'Axis of Evil' could come in under a similar umbrella?

Cynics may point to the cost of the OSCE (but at less than €200 million a year it is a snip compared with waging war), and the issues it has not resolved (of which there are many). They may doubt that those countries threatened by Major-General Vallely's invasion plan would consider such a co-operative approach. There is also the open wound of Israel–Palestine, the fundamental impulse behind so much of the conflict in the region and beyond. But the OSCE did not emerge in auspicious circumstances from the Helsinki Conference of 1975. The mutual enmity of the Cold War protagonists was still at its height, the final round of the arms race still to come, and the West was losing out to the socialist bloc in proxy wars around the world (Indo-China, Lusophone Africa). Do we have the imagination to re-think the war on terror when the outlook is similarly bleak?

We must not leave the re-imagining to national governments and transnational organisations old and new – and indeed without the participation of existing cultural organisations and individuals it is unlikely that we could move very far. Here, then is the role for the British Council and its analogues. If we are claiming, as we have done recently, that the British Council is 'a force for good', then we must be able to apply this force to the major issues of the day – in this case international security. We need to make bold claims for the ways in which our work in promoting cultural understanding contributes to the creation of a more secure world, not just in terms of mutual benefit, but in directly or indirectly reducing the terror threat in the countries where we work. We have already made a beginning, with events like the Representing Islam seminar in June 2003. An event with two central themes: how the West sees Islam and how Muslims see each other, particularly those in the old Muslim heartlands of the Middle East, South and East Asia and the diasporic Muslims of the West. It looked at popular misunderstandings of Islam and how the Western press (mis)represents Muslims.

It is not possible to list the wars we have prevented, or conflicts that never happened thanks to the British Council. But conflict prevention is in our foundation and in our lifeblood. We were set up, 70 years ago, to develop 'soft opposition' to the greatest threat to world peace at that time – the growth of European fascism. We should also look ahead, maybe to 2014, when we will be marking the 100th anniversary of Europe's descent into mass slaughter and barbarism. What will we want to be different, as a result of what the British Council has done? If the British Council had been around in 1904, could we have done things that might have prevented the First World War? Will the world be more secure in 2014, and what will we – as an organisation, as individuals – have done to contribute to this?

Let us not be shy about making well-grounded, big claims for what we can achieve. Our competitors for the public purse have no difficulty in increasing the funds for 'hard security' – the military, security and intelligence services – and we must use the sort of analysis provided in this book to press our case for resources and commitment to the cause of cultural understanding. Our strength is not only in what we do, but how we do it, with a sensitivity to and appreciation of cultural differences. We work with colleagues from diverse cultures and countries, sharing a common vision of a world of peace and prosperity and mutual respect for all.

Much thinking about security and terrorism is based on fear. Fear of the unknown, the unexpected, and the different. Even responsible politicians inflame that fear, and irresponsible newspapers and commentators compound the escalation of fear in people's minds. What we are offering in our approach is not fear, but understanding and hope on the basis that whatever our faith and background, there is more that unites us than divides us. But in the current world, as the introductory quotation from Yeats neatly encapsulates, hope is a weaker currency. It is my hope that these papers and indeed this series of book can expand the intellectual marketplace for understanding and hope.

Should we talk to political Islam?

Alastair Crooke *and* Beverley Milton-Edwards

'Don't be afraid of opposition. Remember, a kite rises against, not with the wind.' Hamilton Wright Mabie

First and foremost, political Islam is regarded as a critique of modernity, both by those inside and outside the faith system. This is a critique fuelled by the realm of ideas, but also by the experience of Muslims living in our rapidly changing modern societies. In focusing their antipathy on processes of modernisation not only in their own Muslim societies but also in those 'modern' Western societies to which they have migrated, Islamists have held the same processes responsible for marginalising and excluding them in an increasingly interconnected world. The common factor is the cultural submission apparently required of Muslims in the face of that monocultural construct known as secularism.

It is hard to deny that Western-delineated secularism, underpinning Western modernisation and assailing Muslim societies through imperial and colonialist expansion and doctrines of national liberation alike, has resulted in the serious erosion, even eradication, of some of the major institutional edifices of Islam.

In response, as a principal component of their alternative vision of modernity, many Islamists have insisted on a reappraisal of secularism. Challenging Western hegemony, Islamist thinkers and activists assert that behind the fiction of the separation of church and state – that central premise of secular democratic governance – lies an undeclared infrastructure of Judaeo-Christian belief. As Dyab

Abou Jahjah puts it: 'Europe is diverse, but the common aspect, recognised worldwide, is the western European Judaeo-Christian heritage. This has both a racial connotation related to being white; and a civilisational claim, Judaeo-Christian in character. Step outside that framework, and diversity is no longer permissible.'[1]

Islamists question the truth of our Western pluralism and the neutrality of our cultural constructs. How should we respond? What if we actually listened to their alternative visions of modernity, mutuality and the need for dialogue? How open is the modernising West to the reform of those values to which we cling within the global public sphere? To date, we have demanded Muslim assimilation into, or integration of, these values. Would it not be better actively to seek a dialogue with political Islam, promoting security through diversity?

The crisis of modernity

Most public realms in modern secular societies do in fact display religious features. Modernity may gloss over the significant relationship between the way we have lived our faith and dominant economic values associated with global capitalism, but it is a link acknowledged by many sociologists of religion. Weberian analysis of the Protestant work ethic and its influence in the formation of capitalism is the best-known case study. But the religious impulse behind colonial expansion, nation-building, and liberal democracy offers more recent examples of the ways in which the Christian faith has been a crucial catalyst of modernity and, in particular, its relationship with, and impact on Muslim domains.

Religion was little in evidence, admittedly, in that archetypal modernising moment when the West demanded that Muslim societies face a stark choice: 'Mecca or mechanisation?' This superficial alternative had major consequences for the way Muslim society developed from traditional to modern modes of production, polity, culture and public life. Islam was accused of engendering a permanently entrenched, monolithic, narrow and conservative tradition that could never rise to the pluralism, liberalism, or democracy that modernity required.

Western ideas of modernity have at their root the positivist belief that as societies that are based on science evolve, they are bound to become more alike. This is nothing more than a chimera for Muslims who regard Western 'universal values' as a thin facade concealing a Christian single path towards a salvation, open to all. Far from being 'value neutral', such salvation embraces everything from democracy to economics, while Muslim rejection of secular democracy is proof positive of Islam's inherent backwardness.

'Mecca or mechanisation?' was, however, always a false dichotomy. Islam has never been immune to the new products, new industrial techniques, and technical innovation that mark the advance of civilisation. What Islamists do resist is the account of a European Enlightenment culminating in the emergence of secularism, materialism and consumerism as the defining features of modern culture. This narrative accommodates neither their experience nor their theology.

Instead, Islamists – modernisers, reformers and fundamentalists alike – commit themselves to a reassertion of Muslim identity. This process in turn reflects the context in which Muslims now find themselves. Since 9/11, there has been a major 'rebranding' of continuing Western claims to hegemony. The 'new and improved' modernity mantra is couched in the rhetoric of Western security interests, and the arguments of democratic protectionism. 'Modernity' is promoted as a necessary prerequisite to political stability, and an instrument in the 'war on terror'. As the global civic order is secularised, the argument goes, rational conduct becomes the norm, leading to greater political stability and the marshalling of forces able to repulse any Islamic extremists seeking to bring religion into the state through violence and revolution.

Deceit and virtue

The Muslim experience of modernity is not unique. Modernity has been experienced by all societies as a traumatic and often violent transition from one mode of social, political, economic and cultural organisation to another. Yet Muslims are singled out by the West as having uniquely failed. The cultural borrowing that has continued to shape these societies is persistently ignored. Meanwhile, various, and often diametrically opposed, responses to modernity have, in aggregate, considerably weakened the institutional structures and checks and balances of Islam. This helped prepare the ground for those who challenged the canon of traditional Islam from a very different perspective.

Over the past century, Islam's modernisers have freed their faith from its institutional strictures. The intellectual free-for-all that has resulted has brought with it an element of volatility, but it has also led to a subversive articulation of modernity based on values that Muslims could espouse: 'Redeeming Islam *because* it was the "other" opened the door for endorsing an alternative road to modernity.'[2]

Islamists point out that for Muslims, colonialism has been the defining experience of Western modernism, followed by the stark contrast between Western claims for democracy and its support for corrupt, ineffective, oppressive and undemocratic regimes. Liberal Western economics have often been blamed for precipitating greater inequalities, exploitation and injustice for the many, and excessive riches for a corrupt few. Muslims in European societies, they point out, experience high levels of unemployment, discrimination and Islamophobic hostility. Modernity, for them, is very far from being a shared experience or an equal opportunity.

Western self-regard, conveniently drawing on its monopoly of 'virtue', has effectively blocked out such complaints as meaningless. But is this right? There is an argument to be made that western policy-makers, governments and corporations have not given adequate thought to the basis of the malfunction of the

Western economic model in so many parts of the globe. The conceit that the problem lies with Muslim resistance and antipathy or 'exceptionalism', is shaky at best. To persist in forcing through a union of economic systems, rather than generating global economic mutuality, may only feed the ethos of countercultures hostile to modernity.

To most Muslims, the modernity on offer often amounts to little more than cultural submission. Muslim resentment at Western injustice has not only radicalised Islam, but has divorced it once again, as in the Middle Ages, from Judaism and Christianity. An Islam humiliated and marginalised has provoked widespread anti-Western feeling among its followers.

Our unwillingness to see or to hear the messages of counter-modernism within a global discourse is a refusal to accept reality. The realities of Muslim experience and their complaints of double standards can be ignored only because the West buries its head in a single, linear narrative of progress, which sees nations on a temporal continuum from 'backward' to 'advanced'. The West is 'modern' and 'civilised', therefore what we do to advance our vision is benign in intent. Policy-makers may then concentrate their research on the aberrations of Muslim culture, to explain why democracy fails to develop. Western discourse is perceived as 'innocent', too, because of its avowed neutrality. We remain convinced that our separation of state and religion and our economic model of liberal economics, both derived from post-Christian positivism, are so self-evidently benign in intent, that they are the way ahead for everyone, and that those who challenge it must simply be counted hostile to us. If it is hostility that animates them, why look further at what they are saying?

Countermodernism
The United States, in the aftermath of its victory in the Cold War, and with US Christian fundamentalism on the rise, wishes to assert its

vision of modernity, but now as a US security demand. This counter-modernist agenda is seen by the US as a potentially dangerous threat. This is premature. By no means all of the directions in which the project of political Islam, in its many varieties, may veer as events unfold will necessarily be hostile to the West or its values. Without doubt, however, the West's choice of response will play a decisive part in determining which of these paths are taken.

There are potentially positive developments. Strands of Islamism reject polarising *salafi* theories in favour of a more gradualist approach, and in deference to one that works with the grain of popular sentiment. Important debates on governance, popular participation in governance, pluralism and the rights of women are taking place. Within Islamism there is a vigorous exchange on feminism, for example. These are all areas in which, to cultivate security, areas of mutual agreement might be explored. Many Muslims now clearly harbour some sympathy for a more flexible reinterpretation of tradition, coupled with the ability to pose a cultural and political 'Other' to the discourses of the West.

If the mission of global democracy is to succeed, however, we need to do more than simply repeat our vision of it in an ever-louder voice. We are not setting out to understand some obscure 'other' discourse, emanating from a civilisation terminally different from our own. We must open ourselves up to hearing the evidence of the Muslim experience of modernity under Western domination.

This involves an acceptance of a global space characterised by the principle of simultaneity. Those involved in dialogue on all sides must listen in a way that allows their own values to be challenged and, where necessary, modified. Of one thing we can be sure: if there is no space for this in Islam's dialogue with the West, and no acceptance by the West of a different narrative, culture and experience, global democracy will never be the outcome.

In practical terms, we must discard the fiction that as the rest of the world acquires science and becomes modern, it is bound to become secular, enlightened and peaceful. We must assume the probability of opposition rather than convergence, and argue the need to practice acceptance. Of course, acceptance of difference over values that are assumed to be universal is deeply problematic, especially when it profoundly challenges embedded cultural assumptions. In the wake of the Western war on, and occupation of, Iraq Muslim communities across Europe have questioned whether multiculturalism is anything more than an empty slogan, re-awakening all the tensions inherent in the relationship between Islam and the West.

Spoilers

Not all Islamists have an interest in this type of dialogue. One objective of 9/11 was not to stimulate debate at all, but to explode intellectual capacity by shock and awe tactics. However, too much focus on those extremist groups whose resentment of Western hypocrisy has pushed them across the Rubicon, may risk losing sight of the larger picture that is the community of Muslim believers. This is a largely literate global community and diaspora that is unlikely either to return to traditional Islam or to allow their Muslim identity to be overwritten by Western secularism and consumerism.

Their only path, in one form or another, is political Islam. In Europe, this constituency with its links to Islam worldwide, could be harnessed to build a safer world. Thinkers such as Tariq Ramadan locate a third way between assimilation and exclusion, embracing principles of dialogue, culture, and identity, which are the fruits of our 'inclusive memory'. An inclusive approach, he maintains, reflects the shared values in Muslim and Western culture, so that stakeholding is mutual rather than one-sided.

Under this impulse, political Islam could, in turn, offer a vision of modern society based on the ethos and culture of Islam. If the West is willing to engage in this exchange, it can be assured of a positive reception.

Cultivating security and democracy

One aim must be to free up the dialogue on global democracy and governance. Another requirement would be to devise cultural mechanisms that can nourish sociability between the actors. Once acknowledgement of and respect for difference becomes a recognised precondition for global democracy, we have to expect diverging values under some headings, and common ground on others. Sociability should be able to draw on an apparatus of zones of contact that can explore those alien cultural values more resistant to ready empathy.

A fragmented, global world needs cultural experts as translators for its own audience as well as on the other side. In addition to translating Western cultural values into a range of signifiers that have some meaning further afield, cultural bodies could usefully undertake to identify for their own policy-makers, those cultural determinants that have provoked countercultures into being, thereby widening their understanding. These same bodies could play a significant role in increasing sociability through dialogue and zones of contact with Muslims within their own countries, as well as within Muslim societies. Cultural links cultivated in these ways, could play a vital role in the infrastructure of global security.

Sociable economics and development

In the past, Western economic development theory was pressed into service to promote political change in the Muslim world. The 'Mecca or mechanisation?' mantra was calculated not only to bring about better economic production; it was also intended as a political tool. Industrialisation, it was argued, led to political institutionalisation; and the displacement of traditional, usually landed, elites. Religion too, it was expected, would recede from its role in public life as the civic order became secularised. This in turn would lead to political stability as rational economic decisions took precedence over religious norms.

Islamic economic theory, by contrast, was firmly tied to culture and identity. Modern Islamic economic theory has emerged in step with the upheavals wrought by Western economic modernisation projects in Asia and the Middle East. Some Islamists believed that 'if economic choice is considered a secular activity, economic advances will make Muslim existence look increasingly secular. But if it is considered a religious activity, then economic modernisation need not reduce Islam's perceived role in the lives of Muslims.'[3] Bringing economics into the equation with religion was seen as central to the goal of defining a self-contained Islamic order. But Islamists also realised that modernity had an economic dimension that could be scrutinised by Islam and made relevant to the incipient debate about Muslim identity and culture. This provided a welcome opportunity to highlight the universal reach of Islam.

Of course modern Islamist economic theory is also influenced by certain touchstones, sourced in the experiences of the Prophet. These experiences: flight, persecution, rejection of old tribal and status issues, and spiritual submission, have been interpreted as centring on principles of both social and economic justice. Such egalitarian strains inevitably have an impact on Islamic economic theory, and have found resonance among Muslim communities the world over.

The emphasis on social and economic justice has been undeniable in much of modern Shi'a thinking, for example. This, in turn, has been linked to a Shi'ite political agenda that focuses on the underclass and their sense of solidarity with the state and the rest of society. Shi'a doctrine, as espoused by thinkers such as Ali Shariati and Musa Sadr, must be seen within a revolutionary milieu that reflects 'third worldism' and its Marxist antecedents.

Islamists have replaced socialists and Marxists in paying attention to Muslim impoverishment as a product of Western globalisation. Many theorists place alongside the calls for economic justice, equality and social harmony, a critique of the injustices, inequality and lack of social harmony in the West. This however, is a polemic that leaves ample space for pragmatism.

Islamists have also sought to distinguish between the products of a modern technological society and capitalist-inspired consumerism; between productive enterprise and a global capitalism that exploits Muslim societies and communities. Islam was born among traders. The success of Islamic banking too is testimony to its ability to adapt. Islamic economic theory need not be estranged from capitalism or globalisation, as long as neither concept remains intimately tied to Westernisation.

Islamist movements such as the Muslim Brotherhood make clear their commitment to the reversal of economic decline and an end to massively low standards of living. Western prescriptions for these ills, however, are fatally compromised in their eyes. They see the capital intensive approach to the manufacture of consumer items destined for the luxury market, as one that aggravates hardship, by increasing disparities within society. They do not, however, turn their backs on productive enterprises that might alleviate the crisis.

If the thrust of Western policy is perceived to be exploitative and likely to exacerbate distributional inequity, it will serve only to increase polarisation. But the West should have no problem in finding zones of sociability with this economic outlook. Modern theories of development no longer designate tradition and cultural inheritance relics from the past, hardly amenable to change or modernity. Tribal, clan, family and religious networks are all now appealed to as possible facilitators of development. Social and political change can be presented in a more acceptable light, because they are legitimated by the progressive reinterpretation of traditional tendencies within Islam that is already under way.

This is well illustrated in Zaki Badawi's approach to the Muslim principle of *zakat* (charity for sanctity) as a form of development finance and ethical economic theory. As Badawi asserts: '*Zakat* funds should plan to achieve the aim of the Shari'a – that is to find a long-term solution to poverty and dependence.'[4]

There is room for dialogue here on how Western economic engagement may be fashioned to work with the grain of Muslim culture and values. Again rather than striving to attain a union between the economic systems of the West and the Muslim world, it may be more productive to acknowledge mutuality and difference.

For neighbouring European states, with their own Muslim citizens, finding zones of sociability in the cultural as well as in the economic spheres may help considerably to lessen political dissent. The idea that as time passes we shall all become more alike and share similar values, is relatively new. It is just as reasonable to expect and plan for the opposite. In the past the response to this was tolerance – broad-mindedness and respect for what was distinct about the Other. This is even more vital as we enter a period where Islam is perceived as increasingly isolated from Christianity and Judaism as well as from other Western cultural norms.

Perhaps the unpalatable truth is that outsiders are unable positively to influence the process of deep institutional and cultural change that alone can overcome the profound crisis facing the Muslim world. By misdiagnosis of the issues, however, the West has played a considerable part in precipitating the crisis.

From dialogue to governance

We have argued that if there is to be any really meaningful dialogue with political Islam, the West needs to accept the role of listening, actively promoting symmetry in dialogue, and being ready to accommodate alternative discourses on the experience of modernity.

We also argue that the underlying Christian optic should be acknowledged – at least to ourselves. Meanwhile, Islamists might usefully attempt to transmute the idealism and energy of the early community of Muslims to the level of the state, large-scale enterprises and institutions, as their contribution to sociability.

There will be some, however, who will doubt the value of dialogue with groups claiming to derive their views from a strict and fundamentalist interpretation of God's will. Dogmatism and inflexibility is associated with any cultural, political, social or economic movement. It is true that when conflict occurs, dialogue becomes all the more difficult, and where it might be seen to reward those responsible, can be ruled out altogether .This should not be an excuse to refuse the attempt.[5]

In the very different circumstance of sustained dialogue with Islamists, in the first instance, we should be trying to listen to another narrative. We must be prepared for the regular mention throughout much Islamist writing of those striking 'parallels of the hostility' with which the West has always greeted Islam. Extending from the inhabitants of Mecca and their allies, through the Crusader knights of Europe in the Middle Ages to the pith-helmeted colonialists of the 18th and 19th centuries and includes the current hostility, from a West whose collective mind appears similarly shut to their mission. Some Islamists argue that this is a struggle principally of faith and rivalry; others believe that once again it will entail a resort to force and self-defence, just as the first community of Muslims was faced with the need to respond to violent organised opposition.

What you will not find, here, is any monolithic ideology. On the contrary, we have argued that the loosening of its internal checks and balances, and jettisoning of much of the traditional canon of Islam has made it once again vulnerable to change. The Qur'an may be viewed as a political document, a blueprint for a system for practical human life in all its aspects but it is silent on specifics at many points. As a result, Islam can be remarkably adaptable. Thus, Eickelman and Piscatori have noted with respect to Muslim law:

'Emendations and additions to a purportedly invariant and complete Islamic Law (shari'a) have occurred throughout Islamic history, particularly since the mid-19th century. Muslim jurists have rigorously maintained the pious fiction that there can be no change in divinely revealed law, even as they have exercised their independent judgement *(ijtihad)* to create a kind of de facto legislation . . . even in such a reputedly conservative country as Saudi Arabia, legal reforms routinely occur, often made possible by the invocation of the 'public interest' as an overriding Islamic concern.'[6]

To cite the immutability of Islam as a reason to desist from dialogue is inadequate, if not seriously flawed. If the more plausible case is made that the Islamists have failed to elaborate either solutions or a well-defined political platform that can face up to the challenges of modern society, then discourse is more – not less – likely to encourage political Islam to define its project in more concrete terms. In the void left by the retreat of the traditional Islamic establishment, the decline of the secular Left and of the nationalist Arab cause, political Islam has become the torchbearer for many Muslims. It is surely worth making the effort to hear what it is that they have to say.

Endnotes

[1] Rosemary Bechler, 'Everyone is afraid: the world according to Abou Jahjah', *Open Democracy*, 20 May 2004.

[2] Susan Buck-Morss, *Thinking past terror: Islamism and critical theory on the left*, London, Verso, 2003, p. 98.

[3] Timur Kamran, 'The genesis of Islamic economics', *Social Research*, vol. 64:2, summer, 1997.

[4] Zaki Badawi, *Zakat: A new source of development finance?* http://ireland.iol.ie/~afifi/Articles/zakat.htm

[5] See: Charles Taylor 'The Politics of Recognition.' in Gutman, A. & Taylor, C. *Multiculturalism: Examining the Politics of Recognition.* Princeton University Press, Princeton, 1994.

[6] D. Eickelman & J. Piscatori, *Muslim Politics*, Princeton University Press, Princeton, 1996.

The Red Zone

Mary Kaldor

Based on a 'Re-imagining security' interview conducted by Rosemary Bechler.

When I returned to Iraq this May, I met with a group of highly qualified professional and activist women that included a journalist; a former diplomat; specialists in international law, human rights, planning and IT; a pharmacologist, an engineer; and an interior designer. The United Nations Development Fund for Women (UNIFEM) programme co-ordinator who was there, told me that it was one of the most vibrant discussions that she had participated in. The subject was the problem of violence unleashed by the war.

I was not surprised by the level or the passion of the debate. Women's movements trying to stop the war have become a familiar aspect of the post-Cold War conflict situations, which I first described as 'new wars' five years ago in *New and Old Wars: organised violence in a global era*. Because civilian casualties are so high in these wars, women and their children are the main victims. The main explanation for the violence, it was agreed, is the humiliation of occupation – the provocation of 'US army units filling Iraqi streets and cities, implementing democracy and freedom by force' as one university professor put it. But there were differing views about why the resistance has taken such a violent form, ranging from the brutalisation of a highly militarised society that in living memory has gone through three major wars and widespread repression, to economic collapse in a globalising world, an ethical vacuum, and domestic violence. As usual, everyone had something to say – the thirst for debate and discussion and the opening up of an active civil society, which is perhaps the most encouraging sign of all.

I took part in several similar meetings with a whole range of Iraqi civil society groups. I found that the most useful way of provoking discussion was to begin with this fundamental shift in the logic of war. To summarise the difference: an old war is a war between states, for state interest, where the protagonists are armed forces and the decisive moment is battle. A new war, by contrast, is one of state disintegration, fought by a mixture of state and non-state actors. It feeds off identity politics, that is, identities constructed around ethnicity or religion; and it is financed, not through taxation, but various kinds of criminal activity. Approached in these terms, the Iran–Iraq war could be described as the last of the old wars, and indeed as an anachronistic throwback to the First World War, with which it had much in common. By the Second World War, it was much more evident that military technology had become so deadly that if you pit armies against each other, the result is a stalemate. For a brief time in the Second World War, that stalemate was breached with aircraft and tanks. But these, in turn, are now as vulnerable as people, in a war between symmetrical opponents.

When it went to war with Iraq in 2003, the United States had in mind an old war scenario: it could defeat Iraq by toppling the government, and take control. What it did not understand was that it would soon find itself instead in a new war situation. The coalition partners received plenty of warnings that they should at least have plans for a difficult aftermath. This was one of the main reasons that people like me were against the war. It is now all too evident that the United States does not control Iraq, but that its occupying forces are there on the basis of the consent of the Iraqi people. Moreover, all the further characteristics of what is now going on are typical features of a new war. Above all, in a new war – it is the same in Palestine, the same in Chechnya and the same, recent reports simply confirm, in Kashmir – the use of classic military means has completely counterproductive consequences. To use military means against an assortment of criminals and insurgents, is simply to provoke and consolidate support for those groups.

My main argument against going to war was that it would provoke terrorism. What is this terrorism if not new war on a global scale, which the 'war on terror' – the classic military response – just feeds and incites? Now, in the difficult aftermath, this may be becoming easier to point out to governments, together with the fact that new wars, unlike old wars, do not have decisive beginnings and decisive endings. Whether the cause of and conditions leading to a new war are low levels of taxation, the existence of private warlords and paramilitary groups, or the strength of ethnic sentiment, none of these factors is resolved by the war itself. Quite the reverse. All these factors will have become even more deeply entrenched and exacerbated as a result. So much so that in the end, if you can call it an end, the ceasefire is merely a truce. There are no military victories in a new war: only, in the long term if you are lucky, a political victory.

The gap in understanding

Had they understood Iraqi culture better, the Americans might never have made a series of terrible mistakes right from the beginning. The US administration was caught up in that brand of cold-war thinking inspired by their proudest moments after the Second World War when, as they see it, they came to Europe, gave it democracy, and led the way in the de-Nazification of Germany. The neo-cons I spoke to before the Iraq conflict often referred to the German and Japanese models, vowing to undertake a similar process in Iraq. The great difference of course, was that this time, they had a tiny force, and were reliant on private contractors. Given these assumptions, it was not surprising that US intelligence relied so heavily on Ahmed Chalabi, who had his own reasons for thinking that the army should be totally disbanded, and for advocating a sweeping de-Ba'athification process.

In *New and Old Wars*, I argued that crucial to the control of violence under such circumstances is the reconstruction of legitimacy, and called for a new form of 'cosmopolitan political mobilisation', embracing both the so-called international community and local populations, capable of countering the submission to various types of particularism. The reverse of this situation is what has been playing itself out in Iraq in recent months. Last November, many people, even those who opposed the war, believed that the presence of coalition troops was necessary to contain the violence. Six months later nearly everyone, including those who supported the war, saw them as part of the problem, contributing to insecurity.

A stark symbol of this failure is the alarming division that has opened up between the Green Zone and the Red Zone. The Green Zone is the heavily protected suburb of Baghdad where the Coalition Provisional Authority is based. It is an attractive, green suburb with palaces and fountains, palm trees and grass. Its occupants are not really allowed to venture outside. So there they are, sitting inside the Green Zone, busily planning the future of Iraq, surrounded by notices saying: 'What have you done for Iraq today?' Outside is the real Iraq, which they call the Red Zone.

The real Iraq is this busy place with lots of things going on – good and bad. I saw considerable economic activity. There was plenty of shopping, with one street brimful of air conditioners ready for summer sales. There is a lot of interesting political debate on every level, concerning the future of Iraq. But there is also a great deal of violence. It was very hot while we were there, and normally the kids would go swimming in the evening, but the people I went to dinner with did not dare allow this in case of kidnapping. There is nothing unusual about kidnappings for ransom in times of conflict, but these have a new war stamp upon them. The motivation behind them is mainly economic, but not entirely. Some of the perpetrators have carefully targeted prominent political families: they are also trying to pick off the elite. (This is typical of new war – this mixture of motivations. Leaders who need people to fight for them, for example, will free common criminals from the prisons. Slobodan Milosevic did this in the Balkan War and Saddam Hussein followed suit. Alongside these people, newly at large, who see the war simply as an opportunity for making money, you will find fanatical nationalists; in this case those Islamists who think that this is what they have to do to finance their cause. (After 9/11, this legitimising of loot and plunder as God's will was one of the messages found in papers in the abandoned car in Boston airport.)

There is a huge culture gap between these two zones. People in the Green Zone do not have much of a clue about what is happening in the Red Zone. It is full of consultants who find it difficult to remember which country they are in. Not only this, but when you report back on what you have learned, as often as not, they will tell you that you are mistaken: you haven't talked to x or y, or read the latest poll. This culture gap I would contend is now reproduced on a global scale, and increasingly in all conflict situations. Most leading politicians are now protected by a 'green zone', which enables them to believe what they want to believe about what is going on in the world. The war in Iraq has exposed nothing if not that huge gap in understanding between Bush and Blair on the one hand and global public opinion on the other.

The same happens in other conflict zones I have visited. Internationals go there with the best of intentions. They sit in the capital, and talk to each other. They fly out for weekends, or bits of leave. It is not that I am advocating classic imperialism, but what happens nowadays is not always an improvement. If you went out to India, you went out for life. Now, those who intervene don't know the languages; they don't make friends with local people; they become rather suspicious. Indeed, how can they know what is going on in these societies? And once it starts – this is the danger of the global green zone – it is a vicious circle. The American administration believed the people whose perspective accorded with their own cultural preconceptions. At best, and as a direct result of this emphasis on de-Ba'athification, so far they have really trusted only expatriate Iraqis. They did not attempt to understand what was happening in the last years of Saddam Hussein's regime. There is nothing more calculated to undermine legitimacy.

In Vietnam, American soldiers would leave their bases to go out into what was apparently often referred to not as the Red Zone, but as Indian country, to 'hunt for Indians'. This cultural evocation of their earliest, pioneering days also tells you something about what is happening in Iraq, where essentially they only leave the Green Zone to hunt for insurgents. The result is that many people in Iraq feel deeply affronted. This is a well-educated society, with lots of experts and civil servants. Many of them had no choice but to join the Ba'ath Party, because that was the only possible way to get a job. These people feel humiliated that they are not consulted and not used in expert roles. They are thrilled if you go and talk to them. They see the preferment of people who have inferior qualifications for many urgently needed posts. That does not mean that the expatriates don't sometimes bring very important skills with them. But on the whole it is the people who are there who know how to get things done.

Had they wished, the USA could certainly have talked both to religious groupings such as the Shi'ite Da'wah Party or the Supreme Council for Islamic Revolution in Iraq (SCIRI), or secular groups like the communists, who were very powerful on the ground – and found out what people were thinking. A great deal was going on. From some of the Islamic clergy they would have heard about the bitter lessons learned from successive failed coups, and new attempts to unite religious groupings in isolating Saddam Hussein. The same religious leaders, of course, are convinced that the USA knew about this all the time, and that it was their fear of an Islamic regime successfully ousting and replacing him rather than any democratising impulse, that persuaded them to make their move. This, again, is typical of what happens in these situations. People are quick to believe that the Americans are all-powerful and all-seeing. Whichever way you look at it, what remains glaring is the information gap: the chasm between the zones.

Supporting the democrats

For people in Britain, America and elsewhere, there is plenty to be done to support democrats throughout the world. Indeed, if we do not increase these efforts, we risk reproducing again and again the crisis and the high toll of suffering that is currently happening in Iraq. The underlying cause, for a variety of reasons, is that it is harder and harder to sustain authoritarian states in the modern world.

It is impossible to maintain closed states in a globalising world. Whether you look at eastern Europe opening up in the 1980s, or the Latin American uprisings against military juntas and dictatorships, through trade, through travel, through the internet, people's worldviews are opened up and they become deeply frustrated. We see now what is beginning to happen in Saudi Arabia. There are actually many fewer authoritarian states in the world than there were 20 years ago, and in my opinion all those that remain are under threat. The problem is, as we have seen in Africa and the Balkans, that when authoritarian states are opened up to the outside world, there is nothing automatic about them becoming democratic states. They can just as easily become failing states. And as we are all beginning to realise, that is fantastically dangerous. How then, do you support the process of democracy? The key is to try and provide more space for the democrats to flourish.

This need not mean that we should be pouring economic resources into emergent civil societies and teaching people how to be democrats. The British may be marginally better at these sorts of interventions than their American counterparts. But what one nearly always finds is what I can only describe as a certain kind of institutionalised racism. It sets in when people believe that they have come to teach other people how to do things. I sit on the Westminster Foundation for Democracy as a governor, where I have encountered quite a lot of talk about 'democracy assistance': teaching people how to build democracy. Often these projects are aimed at places and situations where there are very brave democrats and human rights activists who know what needs to be done much better than we do, and who simply want our support. But you cannot build democracy from the outside. If the international community want to help create spaces for civil society, or let us say, for civility, to flourish, this cannot be done artificially. Democracy, when all is said and done, depends on participation, and on people making demands through struggle. You cannot impose this.

Is it engrained in our thinking, this deep lack of respect for people in conflict situations? I remember in the middle of the Bosnian war, proposing to David Owen when he was chairman of the International Committee on the Former Yugoslavia, that I would bring the three most brilliant people I knew from Yugoslavia to talk to him: one from Serbia; one from Bosnia; and one from Croatia. He obviously agreed to see them as a favour to me rather than because he thought it would be useful to him. From Bosnia, Zdravko Grebo, a professor of international law known as 'the conscience of Sarajevo' was flown out by military aeroplane to this appointment. What did David Owen do? He sat there with the three most brilliant people in Yugoslavia who urgently wanted to discuss an international protectorate with him, and he lectured us, turning to Zdravko, who is Muslim by background and married to a Serbian but completely secular, and telling him at one point, 'I have walked around Sarajevo, and seen for myself that there are Muslims and Serbs who live in the same blocks of flats' . . . and so on. They were terribly depressed. Nobody was interested in them.

When I go to places like the Caucasus and Iraq now, I always meet people who are not only very intelligent and well-read, but also incredibly brave; people who ought to be treated with enormous respect. Instead, young people swan in and say, 'you know what you should do is this'. It is very deeply embedded in our culture, this sense that we know better; and it is a form of institutionalised racism. I would say that making friends with the locals in Iraq is talking to the women, talking to the students, talking to the communists. In eastern Europe, we were talking to the human rights activists. In Iraq, the communists are the dissidents. You have to find them wherever they are.

Once you find these sorts of people, it is essential to recognise that they are a major source of intelligence. If we wanted to influence Saddam Hussein, we should have asked the advice of the local communists or the local women's groups about the best way to do it. They are a much better source of intelligence than spies or technical intelligence. Of course, there may be a case for supporting certain groups and providing financial assistance as well, but the principal point is to get local advice about what is important. They may say, as they did in Serbia for example, that the best thing you can do is to support a network of independent radio stations, which costs money. But it makes a great deal of difference if you begin to see this, not as an exercise in 'democracy assistance', but in intelligence and understanding.

If we British are any better at this than the Americans, it is because of our colonial experience, and our experience in Northern Ireland. Over and over again in this history, the British have discovered that military means don't work after all, and that they have got to make friends with the locals. But the British have a characteristic way of doing this. Typically, we look for the local tribal leader. We really do believe in tribal leaders and village chieftains; nationalism and ethnicity is entrenched in our own way of thinking. And indeed, these leaders are important, partly because, offering less of a challenge than ideological opponents, they were constructed as such by the British during the days of Empire. Saddam Hussein pursued the same strategy afterwards. In authoritarian states, rule through tribes, clans and religions is, of course, very typical. It was through the tribes that Saddam Hussein ruled.

Sometimes, we have found ourselves in a lot of trouble as a result. There is a huge problem in Maysan at the moment, where a local warlord who has become a very powerful figure has put his own men into the local police force, insisted on his brother being made governor of the province, and has now been involved in the killing of a local chief of police. Known as the Prince of the Marshes, he was already legendary for having escaped Saddam Hussein's jails, and provoked Saddam into draining the marshes where he hid out. Talking to tribal and religious leaders is still one of the quickest and easiest things to do. But today, they are not the only people you should be talking to. Taking seriously what civil society groups and intellectuals have to say is also essential.

But you have to go further than this. Today, the challenge closely linked to the question of legitimacy, is to start engaging from the bottom up. This is one of the fundamental points we make in a report on human security capacity-building, which Javier Solana has commissioned from us, to be published in the autumn. You have to start from the needs of the people on the ground and how they perceive the situation. But it is easy enough to talk loosely about 'understanding the local culture'. Let us be clear about what we mean. I don't mean different religious practises, culinary or musical tradition or even different values. On the whole, I am repeatedly struck by the extent of shared values among human beings. I mean political culture: people's political histories – who was what and how that worked. You need interlocutors: people who will explain to you what is going on. That is absolutely critical when it comes to the sort of assessment that will allow you to engage in a legitimate way in such situations.

In rethinking global security today, a lot of people are rightly concerned about the issue of trust. But the challenge resides not so much in persuading the Iraqi people, or any other people, to trust 'us'. The principal challenge for the international community under new war circumstances is that we must learn how to trust people in conflict situations to be able to help themselves. A great deal follows from this. For trapped in the global green zone, there is also a huge misunderstanding about the nature of government. Modern government is never about ordering people to do things, or 'getting them done'. It is really all about mobilising people to do things themselves. In our societies, where everything is rather well-established, it is easy for us to take this for granted. We don't recognise it any more. But in a conflict zone, you need people at all levels of society who know how to do things, which just do not get done unless people do them themselves. The job of government is to enable these people – no more and no less.

Consider a good example: Kosovo at a similar stage. Immediately after the intervention, local municipalities were informally set up. In part, the UN operation was heavily influenced by Bosnia, where they had to keep control because of local nationalists. The Albanian part of Mitrovica was quite progressive; the current Prime Minister, a doctor, was mayor. At the time, they were trying to carry out lots of apparently boring but quite essential tasks such as introducing planning regulations – Kosovars were streaming back from Germany and Austria and building houses; introducing traffic lights and traffic codes; or getting rid of the rubbish. (Until very recently when the UN finally said 'All right, this is the job of the Pristina Town Council', there has been no rubbish collection for years in Pristina). In Mitrovica, the UN said: 'We can't do any of that until we have this official joint Serbian–Albanian municipality. We will have to approve everything ourselves.' But they had only one or two people, who didn't have the time. There were traffic accidents, and people gerry-building houses all over the place. It was a disaster.

After this new interim government was announced in Iraq I was struck by the answers I got when I asked various leading actors there, including Sir Jeremy Greenstock, Britain's permanent representative at the UN from 1998–2003, and special representative for Iraq from 2003–04: 'Look, here is a government led by an ex-CIA agent, composed primarily of Ba'athists, ex-Ba'athists and expatriates, with very few Islamists, very few people who actually represent the population. Why do you think this government is going to succeed?' The answer came back: 'It is the most competent government that Iraq has ever had. There are several ministers who have PhDs, and know what's what.' But it doesn't matter how competent these people are, if they don't have local support and a real capacity to mobilise people, nothing is going to happen. This is true of running anything; it is not confined to government.

It has to be said that so far, Iyad Allawi is doing much better than I expected. He is trying hard in some of the areas that will gain him legitimacy, and many, many Iraqis are so longing for peace that they are ready to give him the benefit of the doubt. But the crucial thing he has to do – and whether he will do this, I do not know – is to ask the Americans to withdraw from the cities.

Re-imagining European security
So what impact do these new wars have on the broader European security framework? Robert Kagan has suggested an inexorable divide in the American and European approaches, a divide that of course is only a late reprise of the contrasting worldviews of Hobbes and Kant. The Americans see the world as anarchy, needing a superpower to police it; whereas the Europeans say, no, we have to move towards a rule of law. I am on the European side in this schematic divide. But I do think that we need to be advocating tough or robust multilateralism. We need a common European security policy, because we need to be able to contribute seriously to global and UN operations. Europe cannot simply blame America for abandoning multilateralism, if we are unwilling to strengthen multilateralism by our contribution. We could have real influence if we 'got our act together'.

What should that contribution be? Contributing to global security might well mean providing soldiers. Operations are needed on a large scale. We probably need to be in Darfur, in the Congo, in all kinds of places where things are going horrendously wrong. As an international community, we do have to enforce the law, but in a different way from any proposed by the current American administration. This is where our human security strategy comes in. What we propose in our report to Javier Solana is that a human security force is set up, which comprises military, police and civilians. Using the military in support of law enforcement, whether you are talking about international enforcement or local law enforcement, is a very different role from traditional war-fighting. What you need is a new culture, moving away from a war-fighting mentality but remaining robust. It is possible. What is interesting about Northern Ireland is that the situation forced the British to adjust a lot of the bad military techniques they went in with, to deal with British citizens, because they could not just withdraw. This logic needs to be extended. The heart of any such operation is to be able to provide people with a minimum of physical security. If you are really concerned about establishing democracy or a space for civil society, it is essential that people should be able to speak without fear.

In most parts of the world people are very afraid, and it is that fear which generates extremism and violence. That means taking seriously the idea of global security and of human security – the idea that individuals matter, and that your prime duty is to take care of individuals wherever they may be, no matter whether they are in Britain or in Iraq. This sounds like a rather obvious, noble principle, and of course it is incredibly difficult to put into practice. But if we are to deal with these very difficult new types of conflict, this has to be the starting point. And it changes the way that you act. Values that soldiers have always thought of as important, such as heroism, courage and self-sacrifice, need to be preserved. But they must now be complemented by some civilian values as well, like listening and enabling.

Essential to this new global public service ethos, is a new model of local knowledge. It involves relating to local people and respecting people. Again, this sounds – but is not at all – obvious. Academics at least speak the languages, but often fall into the same trap of being imbued with a top-down approach. If you are taught international relations at the LSE, it still tends to focus on the study of governments and states – 1989 provided a good example of the inevitable result. None of the scholars and think tanks, let alone the politicians, knew what was going to happen in eastern Europe, because they confined themselves to studying the official documents and who was in and who out in the central committees – but we had a good idea in the precursor to the Helsinki Citizens Assembly, the European Nuclear Disarmament (END) movement, because we talked to people on the ground – the dissidents.

In our human security plan, we surround civilian and military planning staff not with classic intelligence people, but people based in different countries who go around talking to people all the time. It is quite a difficult job, as we have already learned from our visits to Iraq, where we fulfilled a similar function. We explored human security in five regions, asking what the EU should be doing. Our idea was to start with the victims and talk to refugees and displaced persons, to see what they had to say. In Brussels in February, we invited civil society people from the regions to meet EU officials in workshops on each of the regions. It was clear that the terribly busy EU officials who swanned in thought: 'Oh these are silly people, and we really talk only to governments because we are an intergovernmental organisation,' but they listened. This major cultural barrier must be overcome. We propose that this be adopted as a permanent technique for the EU.

The challenge human security poses, however, is not confined to the military and government officials. Take business people, who often do know more about what is happening on the ground, but who are always dependent on government contracts. When BP decided to become a human rights company, I tried to introduce them to Azerbaijani human rights activists, and found that many of them were quite resistant to the idea that there were human rights violations and political prisoners in Azerbaijan. They preferred to drive in and out by limousine, talking to governments, and shutting their eyes to the realities. Not employing many locals – this is easy for oil companies.

However, stability is also terribly important to them. Many oil companies were against the war in Iraq, because they feared it might make their sources of supply less, not more, secure. In some of our latest findings on oil and conflict, which will be published in *New and Old Oil Wars*, there is a clear contrast between the past, where an old war enabled you to control the country so that you could extract the oil, which would then be preserved for you by a suitably authoritarian state, and nowadays, where to secure your oil supplies, you have to prevent new wars. This requires a completely different kind of strategy. But since a case was brought against Exxon for being hand in glove with the Indonesian military when they were inflicting horrible human rights violations in Aceh, Shell had its fingers burned in Nigeria, and BP suffered the same in Colombia, it is a strategy companies like BP and Shell and even Exxon, have become very interested in. One of our studies shows how BP completely changed its approach in Casanare, Colombia, adopting what is effectively a human security strategy in order to stabilise the region where they were extracting oil.

There are profound challenges as well, for NGOs and broader forms of solidarity. Organisations like the Helsinki Citizens Assembly, or Conciliation Resources in London, have links with local civil society groups. They can act as a useful guide. But this is not always the case. NGOs are often government or corporate funded, and can be co-opted in ways that make them far less useful. It is recognised that the anti-war movement played a significant role in the Middle East, demonstrating that the West is not a monolith, and disproving Huntington's clash of civilisations hypothesis. At the same time, the movement would have been much more effective had it avoided populism and anti-Americanism and made links with Iraqi civil society, shaping itself into a democracy movement as well. But this takes us back to a debate which began in the 1980s, when the END movement was locked in discussion with the peace movement. It is not going to go away.

The public, through their support, also have a huge role to play in the legitimising of human security interventions. Whether you are talking about Princess Diana and landmines, or seeing people starve on the television, on the whole, any intervention that really helps is popular, even if it is costly. It might even help to legitimise governments. This can be decisive, as it was in Kosovo. Of course, by the same token, we have to be careful about this kind of support. There are very reactionary popular movements: a major influence in the United States today is the diasporas, which are enormously influential, often supporting extremist positions. Look at the Jewish lobby inside the United States, or the powerful Croatian lobby that persuaded Germany to recognise Slovenia and Croatia at the beginning of the Balkans conflict.

Lives risked for humanity
One of the implications of human security that has been most scoffed at in the literature, is the idea of risking your life for humanity. How abstract, people say. I disagree. Once you look beyond the stronger feelings that it is only proper for you to have towards your own family, is the love of nation significantly less abstract than love of humanity? Patriotism is also a constructed idea. And people already do risk their lives for humanity. Ridiculous as it might seem, more human rights activists and journalists get killed around the world today, than soldiers.

Anthony Smith criticises Eric Hobsbawm and others for suggesting that national identity is constructed. He argues that it is prompted by deep cultural attachments, otherwise why should people feel sufficiently passionate to die for their countries? My experience of the Bosnian conflict has made me wonder if we are not dealing with exactly the reverse. In Bosnia, people did not feel very strongly about being Serb, or Croat, or Bosnian initially – until they started dying. A

Serbian friend once said to me: 'This war had to be so bloody because we didn't hate each other.' Could it be that once you have died, people who care about you have to justify this to themselves. Your sacrifice and loss has to have been for something important, otherwise it is unbearable. If I am right, we don't go to war because we are strong patriots, but if it is a successful war, it will create that effect. The idea of the Soviet Union, for example, was really forged in the Second World War. Twenty million people died for it . . .

These were incredibly bloody wars. In the modern era, if we are going to risk our lives for humanity, thankfully, it will not be on anything like the same scale. We are talking about law enforcement. You can never talk lightly about people having to die. But think how we admire the firefighters in the twin towers. This is an idea of service that may gradually come more naturally to us. Anyone who saw that documentary drama *Warriors,* which was about soldiers who went to the Balkans thinking that their job must be to protect civilians, will remember how traumatised they felt when that turned out not to be the case. Such values are created through experience. In Javier Solana's study group we have a German general who was commander of the NATO forces in Kosovo, who is completely wedded to this line of thinking; a wonderful marine who led the forces in Sierra Leone with similar convictions. At the moment, one gets the distinct feeling that we are knocking at an open door – values are beginning to change.

The fifth crusade: George Bush and the Christianisation of the war in Iraq

Paul Vallely

'The sword with which we would kill the enemy must pass first through our own hearts.' St Augustine

When President George W. Bush first met Vladimir Putin, the president of Russia, in Slovenia in June 2001, the first thing they talked about was not the failure of communism, the triumph of market capitalism, Star Wars, the instability of the Balkans or the End of History. Rather they spoke about God. 'We'd never met each other,' the American president revealed a year later. 'The first discussion we had was about our personal beliefs.' The American leader fell to musing: 'You know, it's interesting, there is a universal God, in my opinion . . .' Those present when he made the revelation said that the President was clearly moved.[1] It was not a singular occurrence. Bush later invited the visiting president of Macedonia – a fellow Methodist – into his private study, where the two men knelt alongside each other in prayer. Their mutual Christian faith was also a bonding factor for Bush and the British Prime Minister, Tony Blair, though the latter expostulated with incredulous irritation when a television interviewer asked if they too had prayed together. Such incidents offer an important clue regarding the extent to which religion has come to play a significant role in the presidency of George W. Bush.

There is more to this than the matter of one individual's

personal faith, though the story of his religious journey is not without its own significance. George W. Bush was raised by his father and mother as an Episcopalian, the US church, which is closest in theology and institutional temperament to the Church of England, with which it shares membership of the Anglican Communion. He was an altar boy and later a Sunday school teacher. After he married he switched allegiance, adopting his wife's denomination and becoming a Methodist. But his faith seems to have been perfunctory until the age of 39 when, one summer weekend in 1985, America's leading Christian evangelist, Revd Billy Graham, arrived to visit President George Bush senior, at the family compound in Kennebunkport, Maine. It was to be a life-changing encounter for the President's son who was then running a failing oil company and drinking too much. Graham joined the Bush family for a chat around the fireplace. The next day George junior and the famous preacher took a stroll along Walker's Point. 'I knew I was in the presence of a great man,' Bush later wrote in his autobiography. 'I felt drawn to something different. He didn't lecture or admonish; he shared warmth and concern. Billy Graham didn't make you feel guilty. He made you feel loved.'

It was at this point that George Bush junior gave up alcohol and became a born-again Christian. Though he remains a Methodist, his faith has adopted the heavy evangelical accent more usually associated with the Southern Baptists so preponderant in his Bible Belt home state of Texas. The President reads his Bible every morning. He worships at the services led by military chaplains at his country retreat in Camp David, or at impromptu services put together by White House staffers on the presidential plane, Air Force One, or wherever he and his entourage find themselves. Prayer is a constant. The president prays often on the phone with a minister in Texas who is one of his spiritual advisers. Cabinet meetings often begin with a prayer. 'I pray all the time,' he once told Fox News.

All of this is an electoral asset. Some 60 per cent of Americans say it is 'good for the country' for leaders to publicly express their faith, according to a poll in *Newsweek*.[2] Where the Baptist faith of his presidential predecessor, Jimmy Carter, faintly embarrassed his electorate, that of George Bush Jr seems to be more in tune with his times. But this faith is more than personal. It does not simply inspire and motivate one individual in his discourse with his fellow citizens, of all faiths and none. It colours his worldview in a particular way and, more significantly, appears to shape not just his general political outlook but also individual policies and decisions. 'One of the animating principles of this administration is the restoration of the role of faith in the public square,' says Marshall Wittman, the former legislative director for the Christian Coalition, the largest and most active conservative grass-roots political organisation in America. Bush is, he adds, 'perhaps the first modern president who actually sees policy applications' for his faith. Among these have been his initiative to ease federal restrictions on the role faith-based groups can play in providing welfare services in the United States. And his decision that stem-cell research can be funded only by the state if it uses those derived from pre-existing human embryos (rather than creating new ones), reflects a conservative religious instinct on the complex intersection of science and religion. He has not toed the line of the Christian Right on everything – he has demurred on homosexuality and school prayer. But, in the judgment of the former White House spokesman Ari Fleischer: 'Faith influences the president in that it helps make up his character and his judgments, and his policy decisions are based on his character and his judgments.'[3] Nowhere is this more clear than in the war on terror and the invasion of Iraq.

No one would suggest that the the war on Saddam Hussein was religiously motivated. Indeed all the evidence is that the impetus for it derived from the post-Cold War agenda of the neo-conservative hawks who surround Bush – an agenda that pre-dated by some significant time the arrival of George Bush in the president's office.

An attack on Iraq was a strategic priority of many of Bush's advisers long before his administration was ever formed. Donald Rumsfeld, the US Defense Secretary, and his deputy – and one of the neo-conservative group's leading thinkers Paul Wolfowitz – wanted to use the invasion of Iraq to remake the entire Middle East in America's image and interest and secure a reliable source of oil (in 1990 Dick Cheney, then an oil man, now US Vice-President, wrote that: 'Whoever controls the flow of Persian Gulf oil has a stranglehold not only on our economy but also on the other countries of the world as well.')[4] The plan was set out by another Rumsfeld associate, Richard Perle, as long ago as 1996. In *A Clean Break: A New Strategy for Securing the Realm*, a document he co-wrote with the Israeli hawk Benjamin Netanyahu, he called for the elimination of Saddam's regime in Baghdad as a first step towards overthrowing or destabilising the governments of Syria, Lebanon, Saudi Arabia, and Iran; in tandem the Israelis should permanently annex the entire West Bank and Gaza Strip.[5] Two years later a letter was written to President Clinton demanding a full-scale, US-led military drive for 'regime change' in Baghdad. Among the signatories were Perle, Rumsfeld and Wolfowitz. Bill Clinton rejected the idea but, within moments of the September 11 attack on Washington and New York – despite the lack of evidence linking Iraq and 9/11 – the same plan was being put to President Bush.

What had changed was more than the political reality of the post-September 11 world. There was something fundamentally different about the worldview of the man in charge of America's response. One of the striking characteristics of George W. Bush is the extent to which he is perfectly comfortable talking about the world in terms of good and evil. Four months after the September 11 terrorist attacks, in his 2002 State of the Union Address, he came up with the phrase the 'axis of evil' to label three countries – North Korea, Iran and Iraq – whom he judged to be arming to threaten the peace of the world. 'By seeking weapons of mass destruction, these regimes pose a grave and growing danger,' he said in the address. 'They could provide these arms to terrorists, giving them the means to match their hatred. They could attack our allies or attempt to blackmail the United States. In any of these cases, the price of indifference would be catastrophic.' By June, he was even more Manichean, saying: 'We are in a conflict between good and evil and Americans will call evil by its name . . . and we will lead the world in opposing it.'

A crusade against terror

Few in America seemed surprised therefore when, in announcing the US response to the attacks, the President vowed to launch a 'crusade' against terrorism. The word passed by almost unnoticed in America, where it was generally assumed to be a casual metaphor for a vigorous campaign. But in Europe, with its much more prominent Muslim population, alarm bells rang. There it raised the spectre of a large-scale 'clash of civilizations' between Christians and Muslims – to borrow a term popularised by an American academic [6] – a warning that Europeans, with their great experience of Islam, found to be exaggerated and alarmist. There were fears, however, that given a push by individuals as powerful as George Bush, it could become a self-fulfilling prophecy.

The President's use of the word 'crusade', said Soheib Bencheikh, Grand Mufti of the mosque in Marseilles, France, was 'most unfortunate' since 'it recalled the barbarous and unjust military operations against the Muslim world'.[7] In Pakistan the feeling was so strong that a considerable number of Muslims took to the streets in protest. What Bush ignored – or more likely simply did not know – was that in his speeches the terrorist leader Osama bin Laden had repeatedly tried to present the activities of the West in today's Arab world as a return of the Crusades. Nor did he seem to appreciate the extent to which Muslims see the four Crusades [8] as a dark era in history, and one that was heroically resisted by civilised Muslim warriors like Saladin – a view that is largely endorsed by modern Western historians who have presented them as an unholy picture of indiscriminate slaughter, rape and pillage, which included pogroms against Jews as well as against Muslim men, women and children.

Historians have also catalogued the words of the Crusader era. Saint Bernard – from whom the Crusader Frederick Barbarossa received a cross before battle – ruled that killing for Christ was *malecide* not *homicide* (the extermination of injustice, rather than of the unjust and therefore desirable) and pronounced, 'to kill a pagan is to win glory, for it gives glory to Christ'. Among contemporary quotes from Crusaders are comments such as:

> We have set out to march a long way to fight the enemies of God in the East, and behold, before our very eyes are his worst foes, the Jews. They must be dealt with first.

and

> You are the descendants of those who killed and hanged our God. Moreover [God] himself said: 'The day will yet dawn when my children will come and avenge my blood.' We are his children and it is our task to carry out his vengeance upon you, for you showed yourselves obstinate and blasphemous towards him . . . [God] has abandoned you and has turned his radiance towards us and has made us his own.[9]

When the Crusaders entered Jerusalem in July 1099 they went on an orgy of butchery. Some 70,000 men, women and children – the majority of the population – were slaughtered in a holocaust that lasted for three days. Small wonder that Pope John Paul II, at the turn of the millennium, issued an apology for the Crusades in which the Christian cross came to represent what the Archbishop of Canterbury, Rowan Williams, has called 'the language of the powerful, the excuse for oppression, the alibi for atrocity'.[10] And there is something else which is lodged prominently in the Muslim psyche.

Most historians agree that the Crusaders lost. The Christian armies regained Jerusalem on and off, but were eventually beaten back.

In such a context there is more to the casual use of a word like 'crusade' than merely letting loose the doggerel of war. It was part of the black and white vocabulary which the President found rallied Americans behind him at home but which alienated many in the international coalition he sought to build for his 'war on terrorism'. His Secretary of State spent most of the next day trying to repair the damage caused by his boss's ill-thought out remark. His most significant ally Tony Blair was forced to spend much of the next week insisting that 'war on terror' was not a war on Islam. 'The vast majority of decent law-abiding Muslims', he said repeatedly, opposed fanaticism. Bush himself a few days later tried to row back from his Freudian slip by visiting an Islamic centre in Washington where he attempted to assure Americans that: 'the face of terror is not the true faith of Islam. That's not what Islam is all about.'

Yet the President's error was significant, for it exposed several things. It revealed his ignorance of much of the situation into which he was about to launch himself. It showed how his religious worldview had shaped a propensity to see the world in terms of a cosmic battle of good and evil. And it demonstrated how his intoxicating rhetoric, with its shoot-from-the-hip Wild West vocabulary about 'the bad guys' who are 'wanted, dead or alive'[11] prevented him from perceiving the complexity of situations. He might protest that his use of the word crusade was casual and unthinking, but presidents cannot afford to be unthinking in a world where perceptions swiftly become new realities.

A prophet without honour
It soon became clear that there was more to all this than George Bush's much-derided general linguistic carelessness. Despite the row over the 'C' word he then went on to allow his first actual deployment of troops to be branded Operation Infinite Justice – a phrase with

echoes of the Christian concept of 'just war', which also appeared to arrogate to the US President powers of judgement that, as 'infinite', properly belong to God alone. American insensitivity to the feelings of moderate Muslims was confirmed.

It was further inflamed by the pronouncements of many American religious leaders from the Christian Right in the febrile weeks and months following the terrorist attacks on the Twin Towers and the Pentagon. The Revd Jerry Vines, the former president of the Southern Baptist Convention – the nation's largest Protestant denomination, with 15 million members – declared: 'Islam was founded by Mohammed, a demon-possessed paedophile who had 12 wives, and his last one was a nine-year-old girl.' He went on to challenge one of the monotheistic common denominators between Islam, Christianity and Judaism by insisting: 'Allah is not Jehovah either. Jehovah's not going to turn you into a terrorist that'll try to bomb people and take the lives of thousands and thousands of people.' Other well-known conservative preachers spoke in similar vein. Mohammed was 'a terrorist' according to the television evangelist Jerry Falwell, 'an absolute wild-eyed fanatic' and 'a robber and a brigand' according to Pat Robertson, founder of the Christian Coalition. Islam was a religion that was 'wicked, violent and not of the same God', said the Revd Franklin Graham, the son of Billy Graham, and the man who had given the sermon at George Bush's inauguration as President.[12] Such was the concern that all this provoked in the Islamic world that a group of Baptist missionaries working in ten Muslim countries sent a letter home calling for restraint, saying such comments 'heighten animosity toward Christians' and threatened their work and personal safety.

The government of George Bush could not be held accountable for such remarks, though many Muslims around the world made no such distinctions. But what the Bush administration did fail to do was to quash the notion that the invasion of Iraq was to be, among other things, an opportunity for Christian evangelists to attempt to convert

Muslims. In the opening days of the invasion several fundamentalist Christian organisations announced plans to participate in the rebuilding of Iraq, organising Christian welcome wagons stuffed with Bibles and band-aids. Among them was Franklin Graham's organisation, Samaritan's Purse, one of the world's largest Christian relief agencies, which announced it was 'mobilised and poised to assist those affected by the war to liberate Iraq'. This did not augur well. During the first Gulf war, Graham had sent thousands of Arabic-language New Testaments to US troops in Saudi Arabia to pass along to local people, violating Saudi law and an agreement between the two governments that there would be no proselytising. When General Norman Schwarzkopf had a chaplain call Graham to complain, according to *The Christian Science Monitor*, Graham said he was under higher orders.[13]

Nor was Graham alone. The Southern Baptist Convention, the nation's leading proselytiser, announced it was planning a large relief effort in Iraq once the war ended. So did the American Family Association (AFA), whose website carried a pledge 'to help raise money to help the displaced people of Iraq rebuild their lives and let them know that Christians in America care for them and want to help them through their struggle against tyranny'. Alongside it, on the AFA website, was a banner-headline that read, 'Is Islam a Peaceful Religion?' – to which it gave an unequivocal 'No' in answer. To all this the Bush administration merely shrugged its shoulders, saying it had no power to tell private groups what to do. Islam, itself like Christianity, a missionary religion whose believers have the obligation to spread the message of its universal claims, was in no doubt as to what this meant.

As the war progressed the cultural semiotics continued, spreading far beyond the prejudices of the Bible Belt Christian Right. Immediately after the gruesome beheading of Nick Berg, an American hostage in Iraq, was broadcast on the internet – a US Senator, John McCain, was one of the first to condemn it.

Those who did it were 'barbarians', he said. It was as revealing a choice of word from the lexicon of disgust, as was George Bush's earlier reference to the Crusades. The barbarians were the mindless, valueless hordes who lusted only after wanton destruction against the Roman Empire, the bastion of civilised values. History, of course, shows another side; the Romans were arrogant and decadent and blind to the culture of others. Mindful of photographs of US soldiers setting dogs on Iraqi prisoners, we might recall that the Romans also set animals on their prisoners, and called that the Games. That the war was seen as a clash of symbols was apparent from the other side. Berg's assassins had clad him in Guantánamo orange for his online execution.

More mainstream Christian leaders played a part in the religious polarisation that set in. A former Archbishop of Canterbury, George Carey, delivered a series of politically naïve lectures on Islam in Rome and in Britain. In them, despite his plenteous affirmations of goodwill to Islam, he insulted Muslims by saying that the Prophet Mohammed was acknowledged by all to have been an illiterate and that 'no great invention has come for many hundreds of years from Muslim countries'.

Roman Catholicism offered little better. It chose this time to beatify a friar best remembered for his role in the last Christian Crusade against Islam, Father Marco d'Aviano, a man whom one critic described as 'the Osama bin Laden of his time' whose outbursts against Islam and the Turks were both racist and provocative. The Vatican responded that d'Aviano was a man of peace who had aided the legitimate defence of Christianity against aggressors – which is pretty much what many in the Muslim world say about bin Laden. Rome also incensed Muslims by refusing to condemn the French government's ban on Muslim headscarves in French schools, with one leading churchman, Cardinal Karl Lehmann, in remarks sanctioned by the Vatican, declaring that many considered the headscarf to be a symbol of discrimination whereas 'Christian crosses and religious clothing have not the slightest trace of political propaganda about them'. The Vatican-approved Jesuit journal *La Civiltà Cattolica* also accused Islam of showing a 'warlike face' throughout history. All of which marked a departure from the Vatican's previous policy of simultaneously stressing both positive and negative aspects of Muslim–Christian relations. The message that many Muslims read between the lines was one of religiously-inspired suspicion and hostility.

A Christian army
Such fears were hardly allayed by the person of William G. Boykin. Lieutenant General William ('Jerry') Boykin is the all-American hero.[14] His 32 years in the US army included two stints as commander of the secret commando group, Delta Force. He is the archetypal tough guy. As a captain in 1980, Boykin was part of the abortive attempt to rescue the 53 American hostages held by Iran, a secret mission that ended in flames at Desert One, with the death of eight US servicemen. Three years later, as a major, he helped invade Grenada. In 1992, as a colonel, he led the manhunt in Colombia for drug lord Pablo Escobar, who was killed in circumstances shrouded in secrecy but in which Boykin was said to have played a significant part. He was the man who advised on what kind of gas to use to end the siege in Waco, Texas. But what marked him most was an incident in October 1993 in downtown Mogadishu. Under his command 18 soldiers died in an effort to snatch a Somali warlord, which the US nation came to know in detail through the book and film *Black Hawk Down*. He went on to become the nation's top uniformed intelligence officer. In October 2003 he was the Deputy Undersecretary of Defense for Intelligence.

What brought him to public attention in that month was a story in the *Los Angeles Times,* which reported that Boykin had been regularly appearing at Sunday morning evangelical revivals, in full military uniform.[15] At one, in Daytona Beach, Florida, in January 2003, speaking about the notorious Black Hawk Down fiasco nearly a decade earlier, Boykin revealed that he had collapsed in his bunk that day, angry that God had let him down. It had provoked a spiritual crisis. 'There is no God,' Boykin raged. 'If there was a God, he would have been here to protect my soldiers.' But in the same address, Boykin says he heard God answer him: 'If there is no God, there is no hope.' And he was thunderstruck by the insight that his battle with the warlord was between good and evil; between the true God and the false one: 'I knew that my God was bigger than his. I knew that my God was a real God and his was an idol'.[16] He went on at these meetings repeatedly to describe America's wars in Iraq and Afghanistan as a Christian Holy Crusade against Islam, a religion he suggested was aligned with Satan. Particular controversy was sparked by his remarks to a congregation in Oregon that 'Satan wants to destroy this nation, he wants to destroy us as a nation, and he wants to destroy us as a Christian army'.[17]

American Muslim groups were outraged and called on President Bush to fire Boykin, a demand echoed by sections of secular opinion in both the press and in Congress. But the administration stuck by their man. Boykin was, said Defense Secretary Rumsfeld, 'an officer that has an outstanding record in the United States armed forces'.[18] He had no intention of moving his man from this critical job. Six months later it was to become clear exactly why. In May 2004 it emerged that Boykin was at the heart of a secret operation, on Rumsfeld's orders, to extend the 'stress and duress' methods of interrogation used on al-Qa'ida suspects at Guantánamo Bay to Iraqi detainees inside Baghdad's Abu Ghraib prison.

Doomsday scenarios
Before that, however, there was another twist in the tale of the Christianisation of the war on Iraq. In May 2004 the minutes of a secret meeting between Christian fundamentalists and White

House officials were leaked to the New York newspaper *The Village Voice*.[19] The notes showed that the religious hardliners had met the President on 25 March 2004 and held a two-hour meeting with White House staffers including the National Security Council's top Middle East aide, Elliott Abrams. The apocalyptic Christians, the paper reported, were eager to ensure that American policy on Israel and Iraq conformed to their sectarian doomsday scenarios.

The group, the Apostolic Congress, which claims to be 'the Christian Voice in the Nation's Capital', is an important part of the Christian Zionist lobby that supports the state of Israel and whose members vociferously oppose the idea of a Palestinian state. Their politics have a distinct theological undergirding that insists that until Israel is intact Christ cannot return to earth for the Second Coming. Essential to this is the belief that the great Jewish Temple in Jerusalem, which was destroyed by the Babylonians in 586 BC and again by the Romans in AD 70, must be rebuilt for a third time so that the Messiah can return to reinstate Mosaic animal sacrifices there. The trouble is that the site of the Temple is now occupied by the al-Aqsa Mosque – after Mecca and Medina, the holiest site in Islam. Because of this, apocalyptic Christians believe, conflict with Muslims is both necessary and desirable. These 'End-Timers', as they are known, also believe that the Battle of Armageddon – which will take place on the plains of Israel between Mount Megiddo and the Valley of Armageddon in the north, and Bozrah in Edom in the south – will be brought about by hostile forces mounting a massive attack on the state of Israel. They also hold that true-believers will not be part of this final conflagration but will be 'raptured' and lifted into heaven by the returning Christ before the apocalyptic battle of Armageddon is joined.

The detail here is significant. For they also believe that the Second Coming will finally come to pass in the generation immediately following Israel's re-emergence as a nation; which is why for many fundamentalist leaders, support for Israel has moved to the very top of their agenda. Thus since 1948, fundamentalists have encouraged the continued military and economic funding of Israel by the United States. They back Israeli government policy virtually without question, fervently supporting Israel's sovereignty over the West Bank because God's granting of the Holy Land to the biblical patriarchs (Genesis 15: 18–20) was irrevocable. They urge Israelis to resist negotiating land for peace and instead, maintain the policy of building settlements and incorporating the Occupied Territories within the State of Israel.

A Chosen People

If such a theological position sounds extreme, it is by no means confined to a tiny minority. There are as many as eight million pre-millennial Christians in America influenced by this strong fundamentalist dynamic for whom Armageddon is always just around the corner. Their mindset has had a creeping influence on the way mainstream America thinks about the world.

The result of this belief, on the ground, is to be seen in e-mail chains, prayer ministries and grass-roots efforts to get the word out that the USA must stand united with its ally in the war on terror. Christian groups are spending millions on everything from armoured school buses for Israeli children to halogen lights for the army's emergency rescue service. When the President demanded that Israel withdraw its tanks from the West Bank in 2002 the White House reportedly received 100,000 angry e-mails from Christian conservatives. Since more than 15 per cent of the American electorate describe themselves as Christian conservatives – contrasted with just the half a per cent who constitute the 'Jewish vote' – many in Washington now believe that fundamentalism is the bigger influence on US policy in Israel. Nor are their views confined to Israel. Many of these fundamentalists believe that much of the Book of Revelation, in which Christianity's great enemy is symbolically characterised as Babylon, is destined to take place in the country that is modern-day Iraq.

It is not thought that George W. Bush himself shares the End-Time theological worldview – though his predecessor Ronald Reagan clearly had some sympathy with it; Reagan made explicit references to the belief that the world would end in a fiery Armageddon on half a dozen occasions during his presidency. But if the language of apocalyptic Christianity is absent from George W. Bush's speeches, he has shown himself eager to consult with End-Timers. The leader of the Apostolic Congress, Pentecostal minister Robert G. Upton, has boasted: ' We're in constant contact with the White House . . . I'm briefed at least once a week via the telephone.'[20] And certainly just three weeks after details of the meeting were leaked to the The Village Voice – at which White House officials adopted biblical analysis to argue that, 'the Gaza Strip had no significant Biblical influence such as Joseph's Tomb or Rachel's Tomb and therefore is a piece of land that can be sacrificed for the cause of peace' – Bush reversed long-standing US policy and endorsed Israeli sovereignty over parts of the West Bank, in exchange for Israel's disengagement from the Gaza Strip.

The concern here is not that George W. Bush is discussing policy with people who press right-wing solutions to achieve peace in the Middle East. It is that he is discussing policy with Christians who might not care about peace at all – since peace could slow down the Second Coming, and that in any case they will be saved in the Rapture before the world ends.

The chief anxiety about Bush's application of his faith to his political analysis lies in another important American theological construct – the notion that the United States has a 'manifest destiny' and that its citizens are a Chosen People. This concept of 'chosenness' has long antecedents. The original Chosen People, the Bible tells us, were the Jews. But this special status was appropriated by the Christian Church early in its history, with the justification that the Jews by their behaviour had somehow forfeited this right, which had passed to the Catholic Church. The perception that the Church was especially favoured as the new Zion was a dominating metaphor throughout the medieval period.

After the Reformation a similar sense was growing in Protestants that this chosenness had been transferred to them, as the true inheritors of God's blessing since Rome had lost the prerogative through its errant behaviour. The notion was taken deep into the thinking of English Protestantism and was a formative philosophy in the shaping of Britain as the first modern nation state. But the process was again repeated; after the American War of Independence the former colonists assumed that England has been stripped of its chosenness and that this special status had passed to them.

As Clifford Longley sets out in his book *Chosen People,* which tracks this successionist dynamic in detail,[21] it became a principal component in America's national sense of identity and their self-perception as a people with a right to impose their sense of righteousness on the rest of the world. The implicit assumption is that it is now America that holds a specific covenant with God, who has selected the people of the United States to be his unique instrument, his new Chosen People. This carries with it rewards in the form of political greatness, as well as a moral duty to lead the rest of mankind on the path of redemption. This sense, sometimes unconscious, sometimes overtly articulated, can be detected in everything from the language of radio phone-ins to the political discourse of Capitol Hill. It is most evident in America's messianic born-again Christianity and it is clear in George W. Bush's repeated articulation of his conviction that America is blessed, and God is protecting the country.

A chosen president

This sense has been clear in George W. Bush from the start of his presidency and before, as the following story makes clear:

Shortly after his 1998 re-election as governor of Texas, Republican heavyweights begin to discuss George Bush Jr as a presidential prospect. W. is dubious. Then one day he's sitting in church, Highland Methodist in Dallas, with his mother. The pastor, Mark Craig, preaches on Moses' ambivalence about leading the Israelites out of bondage. ('Sorry, God, I'm busy', the minister has Moses responding. ' I've got a family. I've got sheep to tend. I've got a life.')

Pastor Craig moves on from the allegorical portion of his sermon. The American people are 'starved for leadership,' he says, 'starved for leaders who have ethical and moral courage'. He reminds his congregation: 'It's not always easy or convenient for leaders to step forward. Remember, even Moses had doubts.' Barbara Bush, the high-church Episcopalian whose husband rejected advice to insert scriptural references into his speeches because they made him uncomfortable, tells her son: 'He was talking to you'.[22]

Barbara Bush's use of the pronoun 'he' is ambiguous in this story. She may have been talking about the preacher. But her born-again son does not hear it that way. It is not 'he' that George Bush Jr hears but 'He'. Not long afterwards the born-again politician called his friend, the charismatic television evangelist James Robison and told him: 'I've heard the call. I believe God wants me to run for president.'[23] This sense of personal and national election characterises the whole of Bush's approach. Professor Bruce Lincoln, the author of *Holy Terrors: Thinking About Religion After September 11*, teaches a course on the theology of George W. Bush at the University of Chicago Divinity School. The President, he says, 'does feel that people are called upon by the Divine to undertake certain positions in the world, and undertake certain actions, and to be responsible for certain things. And he makes, I think, quite clear – explicitly in some contexts, and implicitly in a great many others – that he occupies the office by a Divine calling. That God put him there with a sense of purpose.'[24] That purpose, says Bruce Lincoln, holds that 'the USA is the new Israel as God's most favoured nation, and those responsible for the state of America in the world also enjoy special favour'. For Bush to waver would be to tempt God's disfavour. 'Wherever the USA happens to advance something that he can call "freedom", he thinks he's serving God's will.' His habit of ending his speeches with the homiletic, 'May God continue to bless America' suggests, in Lincoln's analysis, that 'Bush and his speechwriters gave serious thought to the phrase and decided to emphatically reaffirm the notion that the United States has enjoyed divine favour throughout its history – moreover, that it deserves said favour insofar as it remains firm in its faith'.

It is a view of the world with which those around the President agree. 'George Bush was not elected by a majority of the voters in the USA', General William Boykin has said. 'He was appointed by God.' It is a small step from that conviction to Boykin's assertion about the US military and its current role in Iraq that: 'We in the Army of God, in the House of God, the Kingdom of God have been raised for such a time as this.'

Abuse in Abu Ghraib

Quite how men like Bush and Boykin reconcile such elevated sentiments with what happened on the ground in Abu Ghraib jail, is not clear. In May 2004 the news broke that abuse bordering on torture was a commonplace in the Baghdad prison in which the US military incarcerated terrorist suspects and common criminals. Photographs hit US television screens, which showed Iraqi prisoners being stripped naked, made to stand and squat without rest, forced to simulate sexual acts, piled in grotesque naked pyramids, set upon by dogs, subjected to mock electrocution and humiliated by being led on a leash on all fours like an animal. Female soldiers with sly grins pointed in ridicule at the prisoners' genitals. The pictures shocked America and outraged the rest of the world. Few Muslims believed the Bush administration's assertion that this was the work of a few isolated, perverted, individual soldiers. Like the gaffes about the Crusades, the anti-Muslim insults of US preachers, the proselytising intent of Christian relief agencies and the comments of General Boykin, they were flashed around the Islamic world and repeatedly shown on its television stations and on the front pages of its newspapers.

The photographs rang particular bells in London at the Medical Foundation for the Care of Victims of Torture, which has dealt with tens of thousands of torture cases over the past three decades. There one of its senior staff, Sherman Carroll, said: 'The idea of it being "a few bad apples" who are responsible for this abuse won't wash. It looks increasingly like a systematic process.'[25] To the experts, the excesses of Abu Ghraib looked horribly familiar, for they echoed techniques of using psychological disorientation rather than inflicting physical pain, which were pioneered in Soviet Russia and China after the Second World War. These included humiliation, hooding, disorientation and depriving prisoners of sleep, warmth, water, food and human dignity. The West came into contact with them when the KGB and Chinese secret police passed them on to the North Koreans during the Korean War – subjecting British prisoners of war to the new torture techniques. British military intelligence, realising how effective they were, applied similar interrogation methods in colonial situations in Kenya, Aden and Cyprus. They were carried over to Northern Ireland too. In 1970 a unit from the British Army's Special Intelligence Wing at Ashford deprived 12 IRA suspects of food and sleep, and placed hoods over their heads, forcing them to lean against walls with only their fingertips while playing into their ears a piercing high-pitch screech of 'white noise'. When the technique became public it was banned by the Heath government in 1971, and the Court of Human Rights in Strasbourg ruled that the practices were inhumane, degrading and unlawful.

In the 1970s, when the Cold War rather than terrorism was seen as the main threat to the West, the tide turned against torture. In 1984 the UN Convention Against Torture and Other Cruel, Inhuman or Degrading Treatment or Punishment was enacted. The international community, with the US State Department at its head, set up operations to monitor torture. The State Department still produces annual reports, with Burma, Egypt, Eritrea, Iran, Israel, Jordan, Libya, Pakistan, Saudi Arabia, Tunisia and Turkey being censured in the latest. But though both the UK and the USA signed up to the Convention both continued to train selected military personnel in the techniques. At Ashford, in Kent, and at a former US base at Chicksands, the tactics are used to train special operations soldiers – the SAS, SBS, pilots, paratroopers, reconnaissance specialists and others who might find themselves behind enemy lines – to prepare them for the possibility of capture. The techniques are, however, subject to a strict 48-hour time limit.

Sexual humiliation, along with stripping naked, is part of the system of ill-treatment and degradation to which the trainees are subjected in the programme, which is called R2I – resistance to interrogation. That the United States employs such techniques on its enemies, too, became apparent in 1997 when two CIA interrogation manuals became public. The theory on which they draw is that detention should prolong the shock of capture by disrupting any continuity in surroundings, habits, appearance and relations with others, on all of which the prisoner's sense of identity depends. 'Detention should be planned to enhance,' one manual says, 'feelings of being cut off from anything known and reassuring.'[26] The emphasis is placed upon psychological rather than physical pain because, as one manual explains: 'The threat of coercion usually weakens or destroys resistance more effectively than coercion itself.' The threat to inflict pain, it says, can trigger fears more damaging than actual pain itself. Though it adds that pain must be inflicted if the prisoner refuses to comply: 'Otherwise, subsequent threats will also prove ineffective.' It also adds that actual pain is likely to produce false confessions, whereas psychological pain is more likely to undermine the prisoner's 'internal motivational strength'.

President Bush in June 2003 denied to the UN High Commissioner for Human Rights that the USA was using torture in Afghanistan,

Guantánamo Bay or Iraq. But in May 2004 his Defense Secretary, Donald Rumsfeld, admitted that methods such as sleep deprivation, dietary changes and making prisoners assume stress positions are being used. Pentagon lawyers, according to the US pressure group Human Rights Watch, have drawn up a 72-point 'matrix' of types of stress to which detainees can be subjected, including: stripping them naked, subjecting them to bright lights or blaring noise, hooding them and exposing them to heat and cold, and binding them in uncomfortable positions. The more stressful techniques must be approved by senior commanders, but all are permitted.

Onward Christian Soldiers

The lawyers' advice, and the matrix allowing 'graduated levels of force', which was drawn up in association with the CIA, are being kept secret. The argument may be that torture conventions do not apply where detainees are formally in the custody of another country. But what is clear is that the advice has created a climate in which US officials and soldiers feel free to deal more harshly with detainees. Nor does it seem coincidental that a battery of 50-odd special 'coercive techniques' was introduced in Iraq in autumn 2003 after Major General Geoffrey Miller took over as US commander in charge of military jails in Baghdad. The general previously ran Guantánamo Bay where, according to one British detainee, naked prostitutes were paraded before inmates to taunt them. The man who briefed him on his transfer to Baghdad was General William G. Boykin.

What became clear in May 2004 was that at the very moment Boykin became mired in such public controversy over the anti-Muslim comments he made while appearing, in full military uniform, at evangelical rallies – he was at the heart of a secret operation in Baghdad. He had flown to Guantánamo (which is known among the US military as 'Gitmo') on Rumsfeld's orders. There Boykin met Major General Geoffrey Miller, the man in charge of Guantánamo's

Camp X-Ray. Boykin ordered Miller to fly to Iraq and extend X-Ray methods to the prison system there. The instruction was to 'Gitmoize' the Abu Ghraib prison.

The revelations about Boykin's role were made in *The New Yorker* magazine by the investigative journalist Seymour Hersh. According to the magazine, General Boykin himself was involved in the design of the military policies that allowed for the use of torture against Muslim prisoners. The implication was that General Boykin, because of his fundamentalist belief in a Christian holy war against Islam, was more inclined to approve dehumanising measures against Muslim prisoners. Hersh claimed that the unit brought 'unconventional methods' to Abu Ghraib as a way of getting better information about Iraqi insurgents and non-existent weapons of mass destruction. But he also reported reservations among some insiders that techniques approved for use against 'high-value terrorist targets' were now being used for 'cab drivers, brothers-in-law, and people pulled off the streets – the sort of prisoners who populate the Iraqi jails'.

Apologists for the harsher regime insist that it stops just short of torture. Human rights campaigners disagree. 'The UN Convention says torture means "any act by which severe pain or suffering, whether physical or mental, is intentionally inflicted on a person for such purposes as obtaining from him or a third person information or a confession",' according to Sherman Carroll of the Medical Foundation for the Care of Victims of Torture. But what also alarms the torture experts is the suspicion that, in Sherman Carroll's words, 'there have clearly been conscious attempts by psychologists to make the techniques culturally relative to a Muslim population'.[27] He pointed particularly to the reports of the enforced simulation of oral sex, forced masturbation and naked human pyramids, which seemed calculated particularly to offend followers of Islam. Other commentators agreed. 'The American public enjoys male nudity – when the men are athletes, actors, or models displayed by fashion photographers for our entertainment – to sell underwear, perfume, sex and other basic American values,' said the Jesuit priest Fr Raymond A. Schroth, professor of humanities at Saint Peter's College, New Jersey. 'Arab men, unlike Western men accustomed to the sports locker room, do not appear naked in the presence of one another . . . these Iraqi men are anonymous, ordinary, dark-skinned, cowering in their disgrace and fear. Theirs is the nakedness of the bombing victim whose clothes have been blasted away, the nakedness of Jesus on the cross. Their nakedness is part of their torture . . . either these men would co-operate with their interrogators, even serve as our spies, or the pictures would be circulated in their home neighbourhoods'.[28] Critics observed that the head of the American defence contracting firm implicated in the torture of Iraqis at Abu Ghraib prison had visited an Israeli 'anti-terror' training camp in the occupied West Bank earlier in the year.

Many will find far-fetched the idea that US officials specifically tailored the 'stress-and-duress' interrogation techniques – which critics dubbed 'torture-lite' – to make them more effective on Muslim detainees. What we do know is that there was an awareness of Islamic cultural differences and sensitivities among the invading forces. A manual for the First US Infantry Division, entitled *Culture Guide to Iraq*, spells out Muslim sensitivities on dress, diet, manners and much else – even if it does so in a way that is ill-informed and patronising (accusing Arabs of paranoia, exaggeration, extremism and of having a black and white view of the world).[29]

Yet even those Muslims who do not detect conspiracy in the US actions are inclined to feel that all this vindicates their view of American culture as carnal, licentious, superficial and amoral. Those US commentators who sought to explain away the Abu Ghraib abuse as rooted in a comparatively harmless cultural form of fraternity humiliation or hazing – the kind of psychology that also spawns reality television – merely confirm Muslim distaste for US culture as debased. When Westerners hear the Islamic dismissal of America as the Great Satan, the tendency is to assume that it is monstrous evil that is being ascribed to the United States. In fact Shai'tan, to Muslims, is not a monster but a rather pathetic creature, a trickster who falls for the lure of cheap materialism, summed up by the casinos of North Tehran under the Shah, when the phrase was coined to symbolise the superficiality of American culture. Shai'tan is, above all, the Great Trivialiser.

Fighting demons

The charge that George Bush has Christianised the war in Iraq is threefold. It stems first from his insufficient knowledge about those he has branded as the enemy. His second weakness is that his religious sense of himself and his nation being Chosen by God dangerously distorts his perception of the reality of the world; so that his norms become absolute norms, his form of government automatically superior to all others, and his spiritual tradition the only really true religion. However forcefully he renounces the word 'crusade', all this reveals that his mentality is exactly aligned with that of the Crusaders. And, third, his intoxication with his own highly charged rhetoric polarises issues in an unhelpful way through a process of demonisation.

Interestingly the UN Secretary General, Kofi Annan, highlighted this very danger in a largely unreported address to a conference this May, entitled 'Naming Evil' and held in Trinity Church, Wall Street, which suffered directly from the horror of the fall of the Twin Towers in New York. Noting that George Bush and his allies had gone under a banner of messiahship, to save Iraq from an evil dictator, he noted: 'Once we classify people as evil it can lead us to do evil ourselves. In fact, we may easily think we are entitled to suppress them.' The demonisation of an enemy – the notion that one country, one people, one culture, can name another people evil – he said is, 'the moral equivalent of declaring war. We cut off dialogue. We absolve ourselves of any obligations to treat them as human beings.'[30] It also gets us off the hook of self-examination. We no longer have to ask what part our own actions may, even in a small way, have contributed to the problem.

In August 2004 an apparently co-ordinated wave of car bombs exploded in Iraq. They were targeted on Christian worshippers at Sunday evening services. At least 11 people were killed and dozens were injured. The incident sent a wave of fear through the country's 750,000 Christians who make up about three per cent of the population. Until this point the Christian minority – who had lived peacefully side-by-side with their Muslim neighbours throughout Saddam's regime – had been largely untouched by violence during the 15-month-old insurgency. But less dramatic forms of intimidation had been evident for some months. Christian leaders complained of kidnappings and murders of Christians and threats against bishops. Islamic radicals had instructed Christians running liquor stores to close them: those who did not comply were beaten. Even before the bombs, several hundred Christian families, who had been relatively free to practise their religion under the former Ba'ath regime, had left the country out of fear of religious persecution at the hands of Islamic extremists.

The main Christian communities in Iraq are not Protestant like the Christians who have been influencing policy in the White House. Rather they are from the ancient Chaldean, Assyrian, Syrian and Armenian churches. Yet after the August bombs one Assyrian Christian said: ' We have seen fanaticism on the rise. We are accused of being collaborators with the "crusader coalition forces".' The next day a group calling itself the Planning And Follow-Up Organisation in Iraq claimed responsibility and said the blasts were in response to the US 'crusader war'. The violence against Iraqi Christians could, of course, merely be part of the general strategy by America's enemies to destabilise Iraqi society. Or perhaps, in the words of the Bible,[31] those who have sown the wind, are now reaping the whirlwind.

Endnotes

1 The private faith of a public man, Francine Kiefer, *The Christian Science Monitor*, 6 September 2002.

2 July 2002.

3 Quotes from Kiefer, op. cit.

4 *The Guardian*, 2 August 2004.

5 The paper written in 1996 by Richard Perle and Douglas Feith fo the Institute for Advanced Strategic and Political Studies, Israel, can be found at www.israeleconomy.org/strat-1.htm

6 Samuel P. Huntingdon, *The Clash Of Civilizations and The Remaking Of World Order*, Touchstone, New York, 1996.

7 Europe Cringes at President Bush's 'Crusade' Against Terrorists, Peter Ford, *The Christian Science Monitor*, 19 September 2001.

8 Historians generally speak of four Crusades, though some church historians have adumbrated eight.

9 Norman Cohn, *The Pursuit of the Millennium*, Oxfrd University Press, 1992.

10 Christmas sermon, 25 December 2003.

11 *New York Times*, 19 September 2001.

12 To be found at www.charitywire.com/charity132/03613.html

13 Plans of some Christians to evangelise as they offer aid pose dilemma for Iraqi rconstruction, Jane Lampman, *The Christian Science Monitor*, 17 April 2003.

14 See 'The Boykin Affair', Mark Thompson, *Time* magazine, 27 October 2003.

15 *Los Angeles Times*, 16 October 2003.

16 CBS News, Washington, 21 May 2004.

17 *The Guardian*, 20 May 2004.

18 Assoiated Press, 16 October 2003.

19 Rick Perlstein, 'The Jesus Landing Pad', *The Village Voice*, New York, 18 May 2004.

[20] Rick Perlstein, 'The Jesus Landing Pad', *The Village Voice*, New York, 18 May 2004.

[21] Clifford Longley, *Chosen People*, Hodder & Stoughton, 2002.

[22] Rick Perlstein, 'The Divine Calm of George W. Bush', *The Village Voice*, New York, 3 May 2004.

[23] Stephen Mansfield, *The Faith of George W. Bush*, Jeremy P. Tarcher, 2003.

[24] Quoted in Rick Perlstein, 'The Divine Calm of George W. Bush', *The Village Voice*, New York, 3 March 2004.

[25] *The Independent*, 14 May 2004.

[26] Quotes are from *Human Resource Exploitation Training Manual – 1983*, a handbook produced by the CIA and used during the early 1980s to teach Latin American security forces how to extract information from prsoners. Leaked to *Harper's* magazine, April 1997.

[27] *The Independent*, 14 May 2004.

[28] In the *National Catholic Reporter*, Kansas City, 4 June 2004.

[29] *Culture Guide to Iraq*, First US Infantry Division, Office of The Assistant Chief Of Staff, G5, Department Of The Army, Unit 26222, Apo Ae 09036.

[30] 'Naming Evil', Trinity Institute's 35th National Conference, New York, 2 to 4 May, 2004, reported by Joan Chittister, OSB, in the *National Catholic Reporter*, Kansas City, 18 May 2004.

[31] Hosea 8:7.

Contributors

Alastair Crooke is former Security Adviser to Javier Solana, the European Union High Representative and Head of Foreign and Security Policy. He played a role in the negotiations to end the Siege of the Church of the Nativity in 2002 and helped facilitate the Palestinian cease-fires of 2002 and 2003. He was also a staff member of the Mitchell Committee that enquired into the causes of the Intifada.

Beverley Milton-Edwards is the author of *Islam and Politics in Palestine* (London: I. B. Tauris), *Islam and Politics in the Contemporary World* (Cambridge: Polity), and *Conflicts in the Middle East since 1945* (London: Routledge) as well as numerous book chapters and journal articles. Dr Milton-Edwards is currently Director of the Centre for the Study of Ethnic Conflict, Queen's University Belfast.

Mary Kaldor is currently Director of the Centre for the Study of Global Governance at the London School of Economics. She has spent her professional life studying globalisation and the transformation of modern warfare. In the 1980s, she helped to co-found European Nuclear Disarmament (END), a non-governmental organisation dedicated to overcoming the Cold War divide. Subsequently, she co-chaired the Helsinki Citizens Assembly, an international consortium of non-governmental organisations promoting global peace and human rights. The author of numerous books on global and European politics, her recent works include *New and Old Wars: Organised Violence in a Global Era* (1999), and *Global Civil Society: An Answer to War* (2003). As Jean Monnet Reader of Contemporary European Studies at the University of Sussex and now in the LSE, she has undertaken research projects for a wide range of bodies, advising governments and international institutions such as the EU, NATO, the Organization for Security and Co-operation in Europe (OSCE) and the UN.

Paul Vallely writes on religion for *The Independent* newspaper, of which he is associate editor. He chaired the Catholic Institute for International Relations for six years; edited a book on the new politics in Catholic social teaching in 1999; and is a columnist with the *Church Times*. Former chair of Traidcraft, the fair trade organisation, for over a decade he covered third world issues for *The Times* and other national newspapers, reporting from all around the world. He was commended as International Reporter of the Year for his reports on the Ethiopian famine of 1984–85 for *The Times*. Having accompanied Bob Geldof on his Live Aid trip across Africa, he co-wrote Geldof's autobiography *Is That It?* He now lives in Manchester. Paul is the author of *Bad Samaritans: First World Ethics and Third World Debt*, (London, and New York, 1990), and *Promised Lands: Stories of Power and Poverty in the Third World* (London, 1992).

James Kennedy has been Director of the British Council in Kazakhstan and Kyrgyzstan for the past three years. He studied modern languages (German and Russian), trained as a teacher of English to speakers of other languages, and worked as a VSO teacher and teacher trainer in Laos and Tanzania before joining the British Council in 1982. With the British Council he has worked in Kuwait, Malaysia, London, Swaziland, Malawi and Manchester, with two main areas of activity – the promotion of UK education in the 1980s, and management of donor-funded projects in education and governance in the 1990s.